HUMILITY

Other Books by Andrew Murray

Abide in Christ
Absolute Surrender
Andrew Murray Devotional
Andrew Murray on Prayer
Andrew Murray on the Holy Spirit
The Blessings of Obedience
The Blood of the Cross
Covenants and Blessings
Daily Experience with God
The Deeper Christian Life
An Exciting New Life
Experiencing the Holy Spirit
Full Life in Christ
God's Best Secrets
God's Plans for You
God's Power for Today
God's Will: Our Dwelling Place
Healing Secrets
The Holiest of All
How to Strengthen Your Faith
The Master's Indwelling
The Ministry of Intercession
The Power of the Blood of Christ
The Practice of God's Presence
Prayer Power
Raising Your Children for Christ
The Secret of God's Presence
The Secret of Intercession
The Secret of Spiritual Strength
Secrets of Authority
The True Vine
Waiting on God
With Christ in the School of Prayer

HUMILITY

THE FEAR OF THE LORD IS THE INSTRUCTION OF WISDOM,
AND BEFORE HONOR IS HUMILITY.

Proverbs 15:33

ANDREW
MURRAY

WHITAKER
HOUSE

Publisher's note:
This new edition from Whitaker House has been updated for the modern reader. Words, expressions, and sentence structure have been revised for clarity and readability.

HUMILITY
Updated Edition

ISBN-13: 978-0-88368-178-7
ISBN-10: 0-88368-178-1
Printed in the United States of America
© 1982 by Whitaker House

1030 Hunt Valley Circle
New Kensington, PA 15068
www.whitakerhouse.com

Library of Congress Cataloging-in-Publication Data
Murray, Andrew, 1828–1917.
Humility / Andrew Murray.—Updated ed.
p.   cm.
Summary: "An exploration of the life and death of Jesus, a discussion of humility as the distinguishing feature of the discipleship of Jesus Christ, and teaching on how to die to self and live for Christ"
—Provided by publisher.
Includes bibliographical references.
ISBN-13: 978-0-88368-178-7 (trade pbk. : alk. paper)
ISBN-10: 0-88368-178-1 (trade pbk. : alk. paper)
1. Humility—Religious aspects—Christianity. I. Title.
BV4647.H8M87 2004
241'.4—dc22   2004027063

4 5 6 7 8 9 10 11 12 13 14 **UI** 15 14 13 12 11 10 09 08 07

Contents

Preface.. 7

1. Humility: The Glory of the Creature 13

2. Humility: The Secret of Redemption 21

3. Humility in the Life of Jesus 29

4. Humility in the Teaching of Jesus 37

5. Humility in the Disciples of Jesus 47

6. Humility in Daily Life.....................................55

7. Humility and Holiness 65

8. Humility and Sin 73

9. Humility and Faith 81

10. Humility and Death to Self............................89

11. Humility and Happiness 97

12. Humility and Exaltation................................ 105

Notes 115

A Prayer for Humility 121

About the Author 125

Preface

Preface

There are three great motives that urge us to humility: it suits one as a creature, as a sinner, and as a believer. The first motive we see in the heavenly hosts, in unfallen man, and in Jesus as the Son of Man. The second motive appeals to us in our fallen state and points out the only way through which we can return to our right place as men and women. In the third motive, we have the mystery of grace, which teaches us that, as we lose ourselves in the overwhelming greatness of redeeming love, humility becomes to us the consummation of everlasting blessedness and adoration.

In our ordinary Christian teaching, the second aspect of man as sinner has been too exclusively put in the foreground. Some have even gone to the extreme of saying that we must keep sinning if we are indeed to remain humble. Others have thought that the strength of self-condemnation is the secret of humility. And the Christian life has suffered loss, because believers have not been distinctly guided to see that nothing is more natural and beautiful and blessed than to be nothing, so that God may be all. It has not been made clear that it is not sin that humbles us most, but grace. It is the soul, led through its sinfulness to be occupied with God in His wonderful glory as God, as Creator and Redeemer, that will truly take the lowest place before Him.

In these meditations I have, for more than one reason, almost exclusively directed attention to the humility that is suitable to us as men and women. It is not only because the connection between humility and sin is already abundantly set forth in all our Christian teaching, but because I believe that for the fullness of the Christian life, it is indispensable that prominence be given to the other aspect. If Jesus is indeed to be our example in His humility, we need to understand the principles in which it was rooted. We need to find the common ground on which we stand with Him, and in which our likeness to Him is to be attained. If we are indeed to be humble, not only before God but toward men—if humility is to be our joy—we must see that it is not just viewed as the mark of shame because of sin. It must also be understood apart from all sin as a covering with the very beauty and blessedness of heaven and of Jesus.

We will see that, just as Jesus found His glory in taking the form of a servant, so also He said to us, *"He that is greatest among you shall be your servant"* (Matt. 23:11). He simply taught us the blessed truth that there is nothing so divine and heavenly as being the servant and helper of all. The faithful servant who recognizes his position finds a real pleasure in supplying the wishes of the master or his guests. When we see that humility is something infinitely deeper than contrition, and accept it as our participation in the life of Jesus, we will begin to learn that it is our true nobility. We will begin to understand that being servants of all is the highest fulfillment of our destiny, as men and women created in the image of God.

When I look back on my own religious experience, or on the church of Christ in the world, I stand amazed at the thought of how seldom humility is sought after as the distinguishing feature of the discipleship of Jesus. In preaching and living, in the daily activities of the home and social life, in the more special fellowship with Christians, in the direction and performance of work for Christ—there is much proof that humility is not considered the cardinal virtue. It is not considered the only root from which the graces can grow, and the one indispensable condition of true fellowship with Jesus. The accusation that those who claim to be seeking the higher holiness have not always done so with increased humility is a call to all earnest Christians to prove that meekness and lowliness of heart are the chief marks by which they follow the meek and humble Lamb of God.

—*Andrew Murray*

chapter 1

———◆———

Humility: The Glory of the Creature

chapter 1

———————◆———————

Humility: The Glory of the Creature

The four and twenty elders...cast their crowns before the
throne, saying, Thou art worthy, O Lord, to receive glory
and honour and power: for thou hast created all things,
and for thy pleasure they are and were created.
— Revelation 4:10–11

When God created the universe, it was with the one objective of showing in it the glory of His love, His wisdom, and His power, and of making man the partaker of His perfection and blessedness. God wished to reveal Himself in and through created beings by communicating to them as much of His own goodness and glory as they were capable of receiving. But this did not mean that man was given something that he could possess in itself, or a certain life or goodness that he could control and use whenever he wanted. By no means.

As God is the ever living, ever present, ever acting One—who upholds all things by the word of His power (Heb. 1:3), and in whom all things exist (Col. 1:17)—the relationship of man to God could only be one of unceasing, absolute, universal dependence. As truly as God by His power once created, so truly by that same power must God, every moment, maintain. Man needs only to look back to the origin of existence, and he will acknowledge that he owes everything to God. Man's chief care, his highest virtue, and his only happiness, now and throughout eternity, is to present himself as an empty vessel in which God can dwell and manifest His power and goodness.

The life God bestows is imparted not once and for all, but each moment continuously, by the unceasing operation of His mighty power. Humility, the place of entire dependence on God, is, from the very nature of things, the first duty and the highest virtue of man. It is the root of every virtue.

> *Humility is the first duty and the highest virtue of man.*

And so pride, or the loss of this humility, is the root of every sin and evil. When the now fallen angels began to look upon themselves with self-satisfaction, they were led to disobedience and were cast down from the light of heaven into outer darkness. When the Serpent breathed the poison of his pride—the desire to be like God, *"knowing good and evil"* (Gen. 3:5)—into the hearts of our first parents, they, too, fell from their high estate into all the wretchedness in which man is now sunk. In all heaven and earth, pride and self-exaltation are the gate and the curse of hell. (See Note A on page 117.)

Hence, it follows that nothing can redeem us but the restoration of our lost humility, the original and only true relationship of man to God. Jesus came to bring humility back to earth, to make us partakers of it, and by it to save us. In heaven, He humbled Himself to become man. The humility we see in Him, He possessed in heaven; it brought Him, and He brought it, from there. Here on earth *"he humbled himself, and became obedient unto death"* (Phil. 2:8). His humility gave His death its value, and so became our redemption. And now the salvation He imparts is nothing less than a communication of His own life and death, His own disposition and spirit. His own humility has become the ground and root of His relationship to God and His redeeming work. Jesus Christ took the place and fulfilled the destiny of man by His life of perfect humility. His humility is our salvation. His salvation is our humility.

And so the lives of the saved ones, of the saints, must bear this stamp of deliverance from sin and full restoration to their original state. Their whole relationship to both God and man must be marked by an all-pervading humility. Without this, there can be no true abiding in God's presence or experience of His favor and the power of His Spirit. Without this, there can be no abiding faith or love or joy or strength. Humility is the only soil in which the graces take root; the lack of humility is the sufficient explanation of every defect and failure. Humility is not so much a grace or virtue along with others; it is the root of all, because it alone assumes the right attitude before God and allows Him as God to do all.

God gave us a sense of reason. Because of this, the truer our insight into the real nature or the absolute need of a command, the fuller and more ready our obedience to it will be. The call to humility has been too little regarded in the church because its true nature and importance have been too little understood. It is not something that we bring to God or that He bestows. It is simply the sense of entire nothingness, which comes when we see how truly God is all, and in which we make way for God to be all. Man must realize that this is the true nobility. He must consent to

Man must consent to be the vessel in which the glory of God manifests itself.

be—with his will, his mind, and his desires—the form and the vessel in which the life and glory of God are to work and manifest themselves. Then he will see that humility is simply acknowledging the truth of his position as man and yielding to God His place.

In the lives of earnest Christians, of those who pursue and profess holiness, humility ought to be the chief mark of their uprightness. It is often said that it is not so. One reason may be that in the teaching and example of the church, humility has never had the place of supreme importance that rightfully belongs to it. This results from the neglect of this truth: that although sin is a powerful motive to humility, there is a motive of still wider and mightier influence—that which makes the angels, that which made Jesus, that which makes the holiest of saints in heaven so humble. That is, that the first and chief mark of the relationship of man with God, the secret of his blessedness, is the humility and nothingness that leaves God free to be all.

I am sure there are many Christians who will confess that their experience has been very much like my own in this—that we had known the Lord for a long time without realizing that meekness and lowliness of heart should be the distinguishing feature of the disciple, as it was of the Master. Such humility is not a thing that will come on its own. It must be made the object of special desire, prayer, faith, and practice. As we study the Word, we will see what very distinct and often repeated instructions Jesus gave His disciples on this point, and how slow they were in understanding Him.

From the beginning, let us admit that there is nothing so natural to man, nothing so insidious and hidden from our sight, nothing so difficult and dangerous, as pride. Let us feel that nothing but a very determined and persevering waiting on God and Christ will disclose how lacking we are in the grace of humility, and how weak we are to obtain what we seek. Let us study the character of Christ until our souls are filled with the love and admiration of His humility. And let us believe that, when we are broken down under a sense of our pride and realize our inability to cast it out, Jesus Christ Himself will give us this grace as a part of His wondrous life within us.

chapter 2

---◆---

Humility: The Secret of Redemption

chapter 2

◆

Humility: The Secret of Redemption

Let this mind be in you, which was also in Christ Jesus:
Who...made himself of no reputation, and took upon him
the form of a servant....He humbled himself, and became
obedient unto death, even the death of the cross.
Wherefore God also hath highly exalted him.
—Philippians 2:5–9

No tree can grow except on the root from which it sprang. Throughout its existence, it can only live with the life that was in the seed that gave it being. This truth, in its application to the first Adam and the second Adam, can greatly help us to understand both the need and the nature of the redemption that is in Jesus.

Man's Need for Redemption

First, let us understand the need for redemption. When the old Serpent—who had been cast out from heaven for his pride, whose whole nature as the Devil was pride—spoke his words of temptation into the ear of Eve, his words carried with them the very poison of hell. And when she listened, and yielded her desire and her will to the prospect of being like God—knowing good and evil—the poison entered into her soul and blood and life. It destroyed forever the blessed humility and dependence on God that would have been our everlasting happiness. Instead of this, her life, and the life of the human race that sprang from her, became corrupted to its very root with that most terrible of all sins and all curses—the poison of Satan's own pride.

All the wretchedness in this world has its origin in what this cursed, hellish pride—either our own, or that of others—has brought us.

> *All suffering and unhappiness is a result of pride.*

All wars and bloodshed among the nations, all selfishness and suffering, all ambitions and jealousies, all broken hearts and embittered lives, with all the daily unhappiness, are a result of this same wicked pride.

It is pride that made redemption necessary. It is from our pride we need, above everything, to be redeemed. And our insight into the need for redemption will largely depend on our knowledge of the terrible nature of the power that has entered our beings.

The power that Satan brought from hell and cast into man's life is working daily—hourly—with mighty power throughout the world. Men suffer from it; they fear and fight and flee it. But they still do not know where it comes from or from whom it gets its terrible power.

Pride has its root and strength in a terrible spiritual power, outside of us as well as within us. We must confess it, deplore it, and be aware of its satanic origin. This may lead us to despair of ever conquering it or casting it out. But it will also lead us all the sooner to that supernatural power in which alone our deliverance is to be found—the redemption of the Lamb of God. The hopeless struggle against the workings of self and pride within us may, indeed, become still more hopeless as we think of the power of darkness behind it all. But eventually, we will better realize and accept the power and life outside of ourselves—the humility of heaven, as brought down by the Lamb of God to cast out Satan and his pride.

Just as we need to look at the first Adam and his fall in order to know the power of the sin within us, we need to know well the second Adam and His power in order to give us an inner life of humility as real and abiding and overmastering as that of pride has been. We have our life from and in Christ as truly, and even more truly, than from and in Adam. We are to walk *"rooted...in him,"* (Col. 2:7), *"holding the Head, from which all the body... increaseth with the increase of God"* (v. 19).

The life of God, which in the incarnation entered human nature, is the root in which we are to stand and grow. The same almighty power that worked there, and from then on to the resurrection, works daily in us. Our one need is to study and know and trust the life that has been revealed in Christ as the life that is now ours. It waits for our consent to gain possession and mastery of our entire beings.

In this context, it is of inconceivable importance that we have a correct understanding of who Christ is. We should properly comprehend what really constitutes Him, the Christ, and especially what may be counted as His chief characteristic—the root and essence of all His character as our Redeemer. There can be only one answer: it is His humility. What is the incarnation but His heavenly humility, His emptying Himself and becoming man? What is His life on earth but humility, His taking the form of a servant? And what is His atonement but humility? *"He humbled himself, and became obedient unto death."* And what is His ascension and His glory, but humility exalted to the throne and crowned with glory? *"He humbled himself....Wherefore God also has highly exalted Him."*

In heaven where He was with the Father, in His birth, in His life, in His death, and in His sitting on the throne, it is all humility; it is nothing but humility. Christ is the humility of God embodied in human nature. He is eternal love humbling itself, clothing itself in the garb of meekness and gentleness, to win and serve and save us. As the love and condescension of God makes Him the benefactor and helper and servant of all, so Jesus is and always will be the incarnate humility. Even in the midst of the throne, He is the meek and lowly Lamb of God.

The Nature of Redemption through Christ

If humility is the root of the tree, its nature must be seen in every branch, leaf, and fruit. If humility is the first, the all-inclusive grace of the life of Jesus, the secret of His atonement, then the health and strength of our spiritual lives will entirely depend upon our putting this grace first, too. We must make humility the chief thing we admire in Him, the chief thing we ask of Him, the one thing for which we sacrifice all else. (See Note B on page 118.)

Is it any wonder that the Christian life is so often feeble and fruitless, when the very root of the Christ-life is neglected, is unknown? Is it any wonder that the joy of salvation is so little felt, when the one thing in which Christ found it and brings it is so little sought? We must seek a humility that rests in nothing less than the end and death of self; that gives up all the honor of men, as Jesus did, to seek the honor that comes from God alone; that absolutely makes and considers itself nothing so that God may be all, so that the Lord alone may be exalted.

> *Humility should be the chief thing we admire in and ask of God.*

Until we seek humility in Christ as our chief joy and welcome it at any price, there is very little hope of a religion that will conquer the world.

How much of the spirit of the meek and lowly Lamb of God do we see around us, in those who are called by His name? Think about all the lack of love; the indifference to the needs, feelings, and weaknesses of others; the sharp and hasty judgments and utterances so often excused by our cries of being upright and honest; the manifestations of temper and irritation; the bitterness and estrangement—all of these have their root in pride. Pride seeks only itself.

Devilish pride creeps in almost everywhere. What would happen if believers were to become permanently guided by the humility of Jesus? Oh, for the humility of Jesus in myself and everyone around me! We must honestly focus our hearts on our own lack of the humility revealed in Christ's life. Only then will we begin to feel what Christ and His salvation truly are.

Dear believer, study the humility of Jesus. This is the secret, the hidden root of your redemption. Sink down into it more deeply day by day. Believe with your whole heart that Christ, whom God has given us, will work in us, making us what the Father wants us to be.

chapter 3

---◆---

Humility in the Life of Jesus

chapter 3

◆

Humility in the Life of Jesus

I am among you as he that serveth.
—Luke 22:27

*I*n the gospel of John, the inner life of our Lord becomes open to us. Jesus spoke frequently of His relationship to the Father, of the motives by which He was guided, and of His consciousness of the power and spirit in which He acted. Though the word *humble* is not written, there is no other place in Scripture where His humility is so clearly revealed.

We have already said that this grace is, in truth, nothing but man's simple consent to let God be all, to surrender himself to God's working alone. In Jesus we will see how both as the Son of God in heaven, and as man on earth, He took the place of entire subordination. He gave God the honor and the glory that are due to Him. And what He taught so often was made true of Himself: *"He that humbleth himself shall be exalted"* (Luke 18:14). *"He humbled himself....Wherefore God also hath highly exalted him"* (Phil. 2:8–9).

Read the words from John's gospel, in which our Lord spoke of His relationship to the Father, and see how unceasingly He used the words *not* and *nothing* of Himself. The *"not I"* (Gal. 2:20), in which Paul expressed his relationship to Christ, is the very spirit of what Christ said of His relationship to the Father.

The Son can do nothing of himself (John 5:19).

I can of mine own self do nothing....My judgment is just; because I seek not mine own will (v. 30).

I receive not honour from men (v. 41).

For I came down from heaven, not to do mine own will (John 6:38).

My doctrine is not mine (John 7:16).

I am not come of myself (v. 28).

I do nothing of myself (John 8:28).

Neither came I of myself, but he sent me (v. 42).

I seek not mine own glory (v. 50).

The words that I speak unto you I speak not of myself [on My own authority] (John 14:10).

The word which ye hear is not mine (v. 24).

These words open to us the deepest roots of Christ's life and work. They tell us how the almighty God was able to work His mighty redemptive work through Him. They show how important Christ considered the state of heart that suited Him as the Son of the Father. They teach us the essential nature and

> *In His teaching, Christ said, "I am nothing; the Father is all."*

life of the redemption that Christ accomplished and now communicates.

Christ was nothing, so that God might be all. He resigned Himself with His will and His powers entirely for the Father to work in Him. Of His own power, His own will, and His own glory, of His whole mission with all His works and His teaching, He said, "It is not I; I am nothing; I have given Myself to the Father to work. I am nothing; the Father is all."

Christ found this life of entire self-renunciation, of absolute submission and dependence upon the Father's will, to be one of perfect peace and joy. He lost nothing by giving everything to God. The Father honored His trust and did everything for Him, and then exalted Him to His own right hand in glory. And because Christ had thus humbled Himself before God, and God was ever before Him, He found it possible to humble Himself before men, too. He was able to be the servant of all. His humility was simply the surrender of Himself to God, to allow the Father to do in Him what He pleased, no matter what men around might say of Him or do to Him.

In this state of mind, in this spirit and disposition, the redemption of Christ has its virtue and effectiveness. We are made partakers of Christ so that God might bring us to this disposition. This is the true self-denial to which our Savior calls us: the acknowledgment that self has nothing good in it except as an empty vessel that God must fill, and also that its claim to be or do anything may not for a moment be allowed. It is in this, above and before everything, that the conformity to Jesus consists. It is the being and doing nothing by ourselves so that God may be all.

Here we have the root and nature of true humility. It is because this is not understood or sought after that our humility is so superficial and so feeble. We must learn of Jesus how He is *"meek and lowly in heart"* (Matt. 11:29). He teaches us where true humility takes its rise and finds its strength—in the knowledge that it is God *"which worketh all in all"* (1 Cor. 12:6), that our place is to yield to Him in perfect resignation and dependence, in full consent to be and to do nothing of ourselves. This is the life Christ came to reveal and to impart—a life in God that comes through death to sin and self.

Feelings that this life is too high for us and beyond our reach must, even more, urge us to seek it in Him. It is the indwelling Christ who will live this life in us, meek and lowly. If we long for this, let us, above everything, seek the holy secret of the knowledge of God's nature as He every moment works all in all. The secret—of which all nature and every person and, above all, every child of God, is to be the witness—is that he is nothing but a vessel, a channel, through which the living God can manifest the riches of His wisdom, power, and goodness. The root of all virtue and grace—of all faith and acceptable worship—is that we know that we have nothing but what we receive, and we bow in deepest humility to wait upon God for it.

Because this humility was not only a temporary sentiment—awakened and brought into exercise whenever He thought of God—but the very spirit of His whole life, Jesus was just as humble in His fellowship with men as with the Father. He considered Himself to be the servant of God for the men whom God made and loved. As a natural consequence, He considered Himself to be the servant of men, so that through Him the Father might do His work of love. He never for a moment thought of seeking His own honor or asserting His power to vindicate Himself. His whole spirit was that of a life yielded to God so that God might work in it. It is not until Christians study the humility of Jesus as the very essence of His redemption, and as the very blessedness of the life of the Son of God, that the void that should be filled with humility becomes a burden. It is not until they study His humility as the only true relationship to the Father, and therefore as that which Jesus must give us if we are to have any part with Him, that

Jesus considered Himself the servant for the men God loves.

the terrible lack of actual, heavenly, manifested humility will become a sorrow. Our ordinary religion should be set aside to secure this, the first and the chief of the marks of Christ within us.

Brother or sister, are you clothed with humility? Look closely at your daily life. Ask Jesus. Ask your friends. Ask the world. And begin to praise God that there is opened up to you in Jesus a heavenly humility that you have hardly known, and through which a heavenly blessedness (which you possibly have never yet tasted) can come into you.

chapter 4

Humility in the Teaching of Jesus

chapter 4

◆

Humility in the Teaching of Jesus

Learn of me; for I am meek and lowly in heart.
—Matthew 11:29

And whosoever will be chief among you, let him be
your servant: Even as the Son of man came not to be
ministered unto, but to minister.
—Matthew 20:27–28

We have seen humility in the life of Christ as He laid open His heart to us. Now let us read His teaching. There we will see how He spoke of it, and how far He expects men, and especially His disciples, to be as humble as He was. Let us carefully study the passages, which I can do little more than quote, to receive the full impression of how often and how earnestly He taught it. It may help us to realize what He asks of us.

What Jesus Taught about Humility

- *The Blessings of Heaven and Earth*

Look at the commencement of His ministry. In the Beatitudes with which the Sermon on the Mount opens, He said, *"Blessed are the poor in spirit: for theirs is the kingdom of heaven....Blessed are the meek: for they shall inherit the earth"* (Matt. 5:3, 5).

> The blessings of heaven and earth are for the lowly.

The very first words of His proclamation of the kingdom of heaven reveal the open gate through which alone we enter. To the poor, who have nothing in themselves, the kingdom comes. For the meek, who seek nothing in themselves, theirs will be the earth. The blessings of heaven and earth are for the lowly. For the heavenly and the earthly life, humility is the secret of blessing.

- *Perfect Rest for the Soul*

"Learn of me; for I am meek and lowly in heart: and ye shall find rest unto your souls" (Matt. 11:29). Jesus offered Himself as Teacher. He told us of the spirit that we find in Him as Teacher—a spirit that we can learn and receive from Him. Meekness and lowliness are the things He offers us; in these we will find perfect rest of soul. Humility is to be our salvation.

- *Greatness in the Kingdom*

The disciples had been disputing who would be the greatest in the kingdom and had agreed to ask the Master (Matt. 18:1). He set a child in their midst and said, *"Whosoever therefore shall humble himself as this little child, the same is greatest in the kingdom of heaven"* (v. 4). The question is indeed a far-reaching one. What will be the chief distinction in the heavenly kingdom? No one but Jesus would have given this answer. The chief glory of heaven, the true heavenly mindedness, the chief of the graces is humility. *"He that is least among you all, the same shall be great"* (Luke 9:48).

• *The Standard of Glory*

The sons of Zebedee had asked Jesus if they might sit on His right and left, the highest places in the kingdom. Jesus said it was not His to give, but the Father's, who would give it to those for whom it was prepared. They must not look or ask for it. Their thought must be of the cup and the baptism of humiliation. And then He added, *"And whosoever will be chief among you, let him be your servant: Even as the Son of man came not to be ministered unto* [to be served], *but to minister* [to serve]." Humility, as it is the mark of Christ the heavenly, will be the one standard of glory in heaven. The lowliest is the nearest to God. The prime position in the church is promised to the humblest.

• *The Only Way to Honor*

Speaking to the multitude and the disciples about the Pharisees and their love of the chief seats, Christ said once again, *"He that is greatest among you shall be your servant"* (Matt. 23:11). Humiliation is the only ladder to honor in God's kingdom.

- *The Self-Abased Are Exalted*

On another occasion, in the house of a Pharisee, He spoke the parable of the guest who would be invited to come up higher (see Luke 14:1–11), and He added, *"For whosoever exalteth himself shall be abased; and he that humbleth himself shall be exalted"* (v. 11). The demand is inalterable; there is no other way. Self-abasement alone will be exalted.

- *Worship in Humility*

After the parable of the Pharisee and the publican, Christ spoke again, *"every one that exalteth himself shall be abased; and he that humbleth himself shall be exalted"* (Luke 18:14). In the temple and presence and worship of God, everything is worthless that is not pervaded by deep, true humility toward God and men.

- *The Essential Element of Discipleship*

After washing the disciples' feet, Jesus said, *"If I then, your Lord and Master, have washed your feet; ye also ought to wash one another's feet"* (John 13:14). The authority of command, example, and every thought, either of obedience or conformity, makes humility the first and most essential element of discipleship.

- *The Path in Which Jesus Walked*

At the Last Supper table, the disciples still disputed who should be greatest, and Jesus said, *"He that is greatest among you, let him be as the younger; and he that is chief, as he that doth serve"* (Luke 22:26). The path in which Jesus walked and which He opened up for us, the power and spirit in which He brought about salvation, and to which He saves us, is the humility that always makes me the servant of all.

Becoming a Servant of All

How little this is preached. How little it is practiced. How little the lack of it is felt or confessed. I do not say, How few reach some recognizable measure of likeness to Jesus in His humility. But rather, How few ever think of making it a distinct object of continual desire or prayer. How little the world has seen it. How little it has been seen even in the inner circle of the church.

"Whoever will be chief among you, let him be your servant." God wants us to believe that Jesus meant this! We all know what the character of a faithful servant or slave implies: devotion to the master's interests, thoughtful study and care to please him, delight in his prosperity and honor and happiness. There have been servants on earth in whom these dispositions have been seen, and to whom the name of servant has never been anything but a glory.

His service is our highest liberty—the liberty from self.

To many of us it has been a new joy in the Christian life to know that we may yield ourselves as servants, as slaves to God, and to find that His service is our highest liberty—the liberty from sin and self. We need now to learn another lesson—that Jesus calls us to be servants of one another, and that, as we accept it heartily, this service will also be a most blessed one. It will be a new and fuller liberty from sin and self. At first it may appear hard; this is only because of your pride, which still considers itself to be something.

If we learn that to be nothing before God is the glory of man, the spirit of Jesus, and the joy of heaven, we will welcome with our whole hearts the discipline we may have in serving even those who try to trouble us. When our own hearts are set upon this, the true sanctification, we will study each word of Jesus concerning humility with new zeal, and no place will be too low for us. No stooping will be too deep, and no service too lowly or too long continued, if we may only fellowship with Him who said, *"I am among you as he that serveth"* (Luke 22:27).

Brothers and sisters, here is the path to the higher life: down, lower down! This was what Jesus always said to the disciples who were thinking of being great in the kingdom and of sitting on His right hand and His left. Do not seek or ask for exaltation; that is God's work. See to it that you abase and humble yourselves, and take no place before God or man but that of servant. That is your work. Let that also be your one purpose and prayer. *"God is faithful"* (1 Cor. 1:9). Just as water always seeks and fills the lowest place, so the moment God finds men abased and empty, His glory and power flow in to exalt and to bless. He who humbles himself (this must be our one care) will be exalted (this is God's care). By His mighty power and in His great love, He will do it.

People sometimes speak as if humility and meekness will rob us of what is noble and bold and manlike. Oh, that everyone would believe that this is the nobility of the kingdom of heaven! If they would only understand that this is the royal spirit that the King of heaven displayed, that this is Godlike, to humble oneself, to become the servant of all! This is the path to the joy and the glory of Christ's presence ever in us, His power ever resting on us.

Jesus, the meek and lowly One, calls us to learn from Him the path to God. Let us study the words we have been reading, until our hearts are filled with the thought, "My one need is humility." And let us believe that what He shows, He gives; what He is, He imparts. As the meek and lowly One, He will come in and dwell in the longing heart.

chapter 5

———◆———

Humility in the Disciples of Jesus

chapter 5

◆

Humility in the Disciples of Jesus

*He that is greatest among you, let him be as the
younger; and he that is chief, as he that doth serve.*
—Luke 22:26

We have studied humility in the person and
teaching of Jesus. Let us now look for it in
the circle of His chosen companions, the
twelve apostles. If we find a lack of it in them, then the
contrast between Christ and men will be brought out
more clearly, and it will help us to appreciate the mighty
change that Pentecost worked in them. It will prove how
real our participation can be in the perfect triumph of
Christ's humility over the pride that Satan breathed into
man in the Garden.

In the Scriptures quoted from the teaching of Jesus,
we have already seen what the occasions were on which
the disciples had proved how entirely lacking they were
in the grace of humility. Once, they had been disputing
about which of them should be the greatest. Another

time, the sons of Zebedee, with their mother, had asked for the first places—the seats on the right hand and the left. And, later on, at the table of the Last Supper, there was again a contention over who should be accounted the greatest.

Not that there were not moments when they indeed humbled themselves before their Lord. So it was with Peter when he cried out, *"Depart from me; for I am a sinful man, O Lord!"* (Luke 5:8). The disciples also fell down and worshipped Him who had stilled the storm (Matt. 14:22–33). But such occasional expressions of humility only bring into stronger contrast the habitual state of their minds. This state was shown in the natural and spontaneous revelation, cited at other times, of the place and the power of self. As we study the meaning of all this, we will learn several important lessons.

Recognizing Our Underlying Pride

First, we learn how much there may be of earnest and active Christianity while humility is still sadly lacking. We see this in the disciples. They had a fervent attachment to Jesus. They had forsaken all for Him. The Father had revealed to them that He was the Christ of God. They believed in Him; they loved Him; they obeyed His commandments. They had forsaken all to follow Him. When others went back, they clung to Him. They were ready to die with Him. But deeper than all this, there was the dark power of pride—the existence and the hideousness of which they were hardly conscious—that had to be slain and cast out before they could be the witnesses of the power of Jesus to save.

It is still the same today. We may find ministers, evangelists, workers, missionaries, and teachers in whom the gifts of the Spirit are visible and abundant, yet they lack the grace of humility. There are those who are the channels of blessing to multitudes, but of whom—when the testing time comes, or when closer fellowship gives fuller knowledge—it is only too painfully obvious that the abiding characteristic of the grace of humility is scarcely to be seen. All this tends to confirm the lesson that humility is one of the chief and highest graces. It is one of the most difficult to attain, and one to which our first and greatest efforts ought to be directed. It is a grace that only comes in power when the fullness of the Spirit makes us partakers of the indwelling Christ and when He lives within us.

> *Humility is one of the highest graces and one of the hardest to attain.*

Putting Off Personal Effort

Second, we learn how weak all external teaching and all personal effort is in the conquering of pride or in the obtaining of a meek and lowly heart. For three years the disciples had been in the training school of Jesus. He had told them that the chief lesson He wished to teach them was, *"Learn from me; for I am meek and lowly in heart"* (Matt. 11:29).

Time after time He had spoken to them, to the Pharisees, to the multitudes, about humility as the only path to the glory of God. He had not only lived before them as the Lamb of God in His divine humility, He had more than once unfolded to them the innermost secret of His life: *"The Son of Man came not to be ministered unto, but to minister"* (Mark 10:45); *"I am among you as he that serveth"* (Luke 22:27).

He had washed their feet and told them they were to follow His example. And yet they had learned little. At the Last Supper, there was still the contention as to who should be greatest. Undoubtedly, they had often tried to learn His lessons and firmly resolved not to grieve Him again—but all in vain. The much-needed lesson is that no outward instruction, not even of Christ Himself—no argument, however convincing; no sense of the beauty of humility, however deep; no personal resolve or effort, however sincere and earnest—can cast out the devil of pride. When Satan casts out Satan, it is only to enter again in a mightier, though more hidden, power. Nothing can avail but that the new nature, in its divine humility, will be revealed in power to take the place of the old. It will become as truly our nature as the old ever was.

> *No personal effort can cast out the devil of pride.*

Taking Hold of the Indwelling Christ

Third, we see that only by the indwelling of Christ in His divine humility do we become truly humble. We have our pride from another, from Adam; we must have our humility from Another, too. Pride is ours, and it rules in us with such terrible power, because it is our self, our very nature. Humility must be ours in the same way; it must be our very self, our very nature. As natural and easy as it has been to be proud, it must be—it will be—to be humble. The promise is, *"Where,"* even in the heart, *"sin abounded, grace did much more abound"* (Rom. 5:20). All Christ's teaching to His disciples, and all their futile efforts, were the necessary preparation for His entering into them in divine power—to give and be in them what He had taught them to desire.

In His death, Christ destroyed the power of the Devil; He put away sin, and He brought about an everlasting redemption. In His resurrection, He received from the Father an entirely new life. It was a life in the power of God, capable of being communicated to men and entering, renewing, and filling their lives with His divine power. In His ascension, He received the Spirit of the Father, through whom He might do what He could not do while on earth. Then He was able to make Himself one with those He loved, and actually live their lives for them, so that they could live before the Father in a humility like His, because it was He Himself who lived and breathed in them. And on the Day of Pentecost He came and took possession. The work of preparation and conviction, the awakening of desire and hope that His teaching had caused, were perfected by the mighty change that Pentecost brought about. And the lives and the epistles of James and Peter and John bear witness that all was changed, and that the spirit of the meek and suffering Jesus indeed had possession of them.

What will we say to these things? I am sure there is more than one class among my readers. There may be some who have never yet thought very much of the matter and cannot at once realize its immense importance as a life question for the church and all its members. There are others who have felt condemned for their shortcomings and have put forth very earnest efforts, only to fail and be discouraged. Others, again, may be able to give joyful testimony of spiritual blessing and power, and yet there has never been the necessary conviction of what those around them still see as lacking. And still others may be able to witness that in regard to this grace, too, the Lord has given deliverance and victory, while He has taught them how much they still need and may expect out of the fullness of Jesus.

To whichever class we may belong, I urge the pressing need for each of us to seek a still deeper conviction of the unique place that humility holds in becoming like Christ. We must understand the utter impossibility of the church or the believer in being what Christ would have them be, as long as His humility is not recognized as His chief glory, His first command, and our highest blessedness. Let us deeply consider how far the disciples were advanced while this grace was still so terribly lacking. Let us pray to God that other gifts may not so satisfy us that we never grasp the fact that the absence of this grace is the secret reason why the power of God cannot do its mighty work. It is only where we, like the Son, truly know and show that we can do nothing of ourselves, that God will do all. When the truth of an indwelling Christ takes the place it claims in the experience of believers, the church will put on her beautiful garments, and humility will be seen in her teachers and members as the beauty of holiness.

chapter 6

———◆———

Humility in Daily Life

chapter 6

◆

Humility in Daily Life

*He that loveth not his brother whom he hath seen, how
can he love God whom he hath not seen?*
—1 John 4:20

What a solemn thought, that our love for God
will be measured by our everyday fellowship
with men and the love it displays. How solemn
that our love for God will be found to be a delusion,
unless its truth is proved in standing the test of daily
life with our fellowmen. It is even so with our humility.
It is easy to think we humble ourselves before God. Yet
humility toward men will be the only sufficient proof
that our humility before God is real. It will be the only
proof that humility has taken up its abode in us and
become our very nature—that we actually, like Christ,
have made ourselves *"of no reputation"* (Phil. 2:7). When
in the presence of God, lowliness of heart has become
not a posture we assume for a time when we think of
Him or pray to Him but the very spirit of our lives, it

will manifest itself in all our behavior toward our fellow-men.

This lesson is one of deep importance. The only humility that is really ours is not that which we try to show before God in prayer, but that which we carry with us in our ordinary conduct. The insignificances of daily life are the tests of eternity because they prove what spirit really possesses us. It is in our most unguarded moments that we really show and see what we are. To know the humble man, to know how the humble man behaves, you must follow him in the common course of daily life.

Is this not what Jesus taught? He taught His lessons of humility when the disciples disputed who should be greatest, when He saw how the Pharisees loved the chief place at feasts and the chief seats in the synagogues, and when He had given the disciples the example of washing their feet. Humility before God is nothing if not proved in humility before men.

Humility before God is proved in humility before men.

It is even so in the teaching of Paul. To the Romans he wrote, *"In honour preferring one another"* (Rom. 12:10), and *"Mind not high things, but condescend to men of low estate. Be not wise in your own conceits"* (v. 16). To the Corinthians: Love, and there is no love without humility as its root, *"vaunteth not itself, is not puffed up,...seeketh not her own, is not easily provoked"* (1 Cor. 13:4–5). To the Galatians: *"By love serve one another"* (Gal. 5:13), and *"Let us not be desirous of vain glory* [conceited], *provoking one another, envying one another"* (v. 26). To the Ephesians, immediately after the three wonderful chapters on the heavenly life: *"Therefore...walk...with all lowliness and meekness, with longsuffering, forbearing one another in love"* (Eph. 4:1–2), and *"Giving thanks always...submitting yourself one to another in the fear of God"* (Eph. 5:20–21). To the Philippians: *"Let nothing be done through strife or vainglory; but in lowliness of mind let each esteem other better than themselves"* (Phil. 2:3); *"Let this mind be in you, which was also in Christ Jesus: who...made himself of no reputation, and took upon him the form of a servant, and...humbled himself"* (vv. 5–8). And to the Colossians: *"Put on...mercies, kindness, humbleness of mind, meekness, longsuffering; forbearing one another, and forgiving one another,...even as Christ forgave you"* (Col. 3:12–13).

It is in our relationships to one another, in our treatment of one another, that the true lowliness of mind and the humility of heart are to be seen. Our humility before God has no value unless it prepares us to reveal the humility of Jesus to our fellowmen. Let us now study humility in daily life in the light of these words.

The humble man seeks at all times to act on the rule, "Prefer one another in honor; serve one another; esteem others as better than oneself; submit yourself one to another." It is often asked, How can we count others better than ourselves when we see that they are far below us in wisdom and in holiness, in natural gifts, or in grace received? The question proves at once how little we understand about real lowliness of mind. True humility comes when, in the light of God, we have seen ourselves to be nothing, have consented to part with and cast away self—to let God be all. The soul that has done this and can say, "I have lost myself in finding You," no longer compares itself with others. It has forever given up every thought of self in God's presence. It meets its fellowman as one who is nothing, and seeks nothing for itself. It is a soul that serves God and, for His sake, serves all. A faithful servant may be wiser than the master, and yet retain the true spirit and posture of the servant.

The humble man looks upon every child of God—even the feeblest and unworthiest—and honors him and prefers him in honor as the son of a King. The spirit of Him who washed the disciples' feet makes it a joy to us to be indeed the least, to be servants one of another.

> *The humble man looks on every child of God as the son of a King.*

The humble man feels no jealousy or envy. He can praise God when others are preferred and blessed before him. He can bear to hear others praised and himself forgotten, because in God's presence he has learned to say with Paul, *"I be nothing"* (2 Cor. 12:11). He has received the spirit of Jesus, who did not please Himself and did not seek His own honor, as the spirit of his life.

Amid what are considered the temptations to impatience and touchiness, to hard thoughts and sharp words—which come from the failings and sins of fellow Christians—the humble man carries the often repeated injunction in his heart, and shows it in his life: *"Forbearing one another, and forgiving one another,...*

even as Christ forgave you" (Col. 3:13). He has learned that in putting on the Lord Jesus, he has put on the heart of compassion, kindness, humility, meekness, and long-suffering (v. 12). Jesus has taken the place of self, and it is not an impossibility to forgive as Jesus forgave. His humility does not consist merely in thoughts or words of self-depreciation, but in a heart of humility. It is a heart encompassed by compassion and kindness, meekness and long-suffering—the sweet and lowly gentleness recognized as the mark of the Lamb of God.

In striving after the higher experiences of the Christian life, the believer is often in danger of aiming at and rejoicing in what one might call the more human virtues. Such virtues are boldness, joy, contempt of the world, zeal, self-sacrifice—even the old Stoics taught and practiced these. Meanwhile, the deeper, gentler, more divine, and more heavenly graces are scarcely thought of or valued. These virtues are those that Jesus first taught upon earth (because He brought them from heaven) those that are more distinctly connected with His cross and the death of self: poverty of spirit, meekness, humility, lowliness. Therefore, let us put on a heart of compassion, kindness, humility, meekness, long-suffering. Let us prove our Christlikeness, not only in our zeal for saving the lost, but in our conduct with all our fellowmen, bearing with and forgiving one another, even as the Lord forgave us (Col. 3:12–13).

Fellow Christians, let us study the biblical portrait of the humble man. And let us ask our fellow believers, and ask the world, whether they recognize in us the likeness to the original. Let us be content with nothing less than taking each of these Scripture verses as the promise of what God will work in us. Let us take them as the revelation in words of what the Spirit of Jesus will give as a birth within us. And let each failure and shortcoming simply urge us to turn humbly and meekly to the meek and lowly Lamb of God. Have full assurance that where He is enthroned in the heart, His humility and gentleness will be one of the streams of living water that flow from within us.*

Once again I repeat what I have said before. I feel deeply that we have very little idea of what the church suffers from the lack of this divine humility—the nothingness that makes room for God to prove His power. It has not been long since a Christian of a humble, loving spirit—acquainted with many mission stations of various societies—expressed his deep sorrow that in some cases the spirit of love and patience was sadly lacking. Men and women, brought close together with others of uncongenial minds, find it hard to bear and to love and to *"keep the unity of the Spirit in the bond of peace"* (Eph. 4:3). And those who should have been fellow-helpers of each other's joy become a hindrance and a weariness. And all for one reason—the lack of the humility that considers itself nothing, that rejoices in becoming and being counted the least, and that only seeks, like Jesus,

---

* "I knew Jesus, and He was very precious to my soul: but I found something in me that would not keep sweet and patient and kind. I did what I could to keep it down, but it was there. I besought Jesus to do something for me, and when I gave Him my will, He came to my heart, and took out all that would not be sweet, all that would not be kind, all that would not be patient, and then He shut the door." —George Foxe

to be the servant, the helper, and the comforter of others, even the lowest and unworthiest.

And what is the reason that men who have joyfully given themselves up for Christ find it so hard to give themselves up for their fellowmen? Is the church not to blame? It has so little taught its members that the humility of Christ is the first of the virtues, the best of all the graces and powers of the Spirit. The church not preached humility as needed and possible nor placed it first as Christ did. But let us not be discouraged. Let the discovery of the lack of this grace stir us to larger expectation from God. Let us look on every brother or sister who irritates or troubles us as God's means of grace. Let us look on him or her as God's instrument for our purification, for our exercise of the humility that Jesus, our Life, breathes within us. And let us have such faith in the all of God and the nothing of self, so that we may, in God's power, seek only to serve one another in love.

chapter 7

---◆---

Humility and Holiness

chapter 7

◆

Humility and Holiness

Which say, "Stand by thyself, come not near me;
for I am holier than thou."
—Isaiah 65:5

W e speak of the Holiness Movement in our times
and praise God for it. We hear a great deal
about seekers after holiness, about those who
profess holiness, about holiness teaching and holiness
meetings. The blessed truths of holiness in Christ, and
holiness by faith are being emphasized as never before.
The great test of whether the holiness we claim to seek
or to attain is truth and life will be whether it produces
an increasing humility in us. In man, humility is the
one thing needed to allow God's holiness to dwell in him
and shine through him. In Jesus, the Holy One of God
who makes us holy, a divine humility was the secret of
His life, His death, and His exaltation. The one infallible test of our holiness will be the humility before God
and men that marks us. Humility is the bloom and the
beauty of holiness.

Humility

The chief mark of counterfeit holiness is its lack of humility. Every seeker after holiness needs to be on his guard, so that, unconsciously, what was begun in the Spirit is not perfected in the flesh (Gal. 3:3), and pride does not creep in where its presence is least expected. *"Two men went up into the temple to pray; the one a Pharisee, and the other a publican* [tax collector]*"* (Luke 18:10). There is no place or position so sacred that the proud man, the *"Pharisee,"* cannot enter. Pride can lift its head in the very temple of God and make His worship the scene of its self-exaltation.

Since the time Christ so exposed his pride, the Pharisee has put on the garb of the publican. The confessor of deep sinfulness, equally with the one who claims the highest holiness, must be on the watch. Just when we are most anxious to have our hearts be the temple of God, we will find the two men coming up to pray. And the publican will find that his danger is not from the Pharisee beside him, who despises him, but from the Pharisee within, who commends and exalts. In God's temple, when we think we are in the Holiest of All, in the presence of His holiness, let us beware of pride. *"Now there was a day when the sons of God came to present themselves before the LORD, and Satan came also among them"* (Job 1:6).

Humility is needed to allow God's holiness to shine through.

"God, I thank thee, that I am not as other men are...or even as this publican" (Luke 18:11). Self finds its cause of complacency in what is just cause for thanksgiving, in the very thanksgiving that we render to God, and in

the very confession that God has done it all. Yes, even in the temple, when the language of penitence and trust in God's mercy alone is heard, the Pharisee may take up the note of praise, and in thanking God be congratulating himself. Pride can clothe itself in the garments of praise or of penitence.

Even when the words *"I am not as other men are"* are openly rejected and condemned, their spirit may too often be found in our feelings and language toward our fellow worshippers and fellowmen. If you want to know if this is really so, just listen to the way in which churches and Christians often speak of one another. How little of the meekness and gentleness of Jesus is to be seen. It is so little remembered that deep humility must be the keynote of what the servants of Jesus say of themselves or each other. Is there not many a church or congregation, many a mission or convention, many a society or committee, even many a mission away in heathendom, where the harmony has been disturbed and the work of God hindered? Is it not because men who are considered Christians have proved in touchiness and haste and impatience, in self-defense and self-assertion, in sharp judgments and unkind words, that they did not each esteem others better than themselves? Is it not because their holiness has in it so little of the meekness of the saints?[*]

_____

[*] "Me is a most exacting personage, requiring the best seat and the highest place for itself, and feeling grievously wounded if its claim is not recognized. Most of the quarrels among Christian workers arise from the clamoring of this gigantic Me. How few of us understand the true secret of taking our seats in the lowest rooms." —Hannah Whitall Smith

In their spiritual history, people may have had times of great humbling and brokenness, but what a different thing this is from being clothed with humility, and from having a humble spirit. How different this is from having that lowliness of mind in which each counts himself the servant of others and so shows forth the very mind that was also in Jesus Christ.

"Come not near me; for I am holier than thou." What a parody on holiness! Jesus the Holy One is the humble One. The holiest will always be the humblest. There is none holy but God (1 Sam. 2:2). We have as much of holiness as we have of God. And according to what we have of God will be our real humility, because humility is nothing but the disappearance of self in the vision that God is all. The holiest will be the humblest. Alas! Though the bare-faced boasting Jew of the days of Isaiah is not often to be found—even our manners have taught us not to speak in this way—how often his spirit is still seen, whether in the treatment of fellow believers or of the men and women of the world. In the spirit in which opinions are given, work is undertaken, and faults are exposed, how often the voice is still that of the Pharisee, though the garb is that of the publican: *"God, I thank thee, that I am not as other men are"* (Luke 18:11).

Is there, then, any humility to be found, such that men will indeed still consider themselves *"less than the least of all saints"* (Eph. 3:8), the servants of all? There is. Love *"vaunteth not itself, is not puffed up,...seeketh not her own"* (1 Cor. 13:4–5). The power of a perfect love forgets itself and finds its blessedness in blessing others—in bearing with and honoring them, however feeble they may be. The power of this love is given where the spirit of love is poured out in the heart (Rom. 5:5), where the divine nature comes to a full birth, and where Christ, the *"meek and lowly"* (Matt. 11:29) Lamb of God, is truly formed within. Where this love enters, God enters. And where God has entered in His power and reveals Himself as all, man becomes nothing. And where man becomes nothing before God, he cannot be anything but humble toward his fellowmen. The presence of God becomes not a thing of times and seasons, but the covering under which the soul always dwells. Its deep humility before God becomes the holy place of His presence from which all its words and works proceed.

May God teach us that our thoughts and words and feelings concerning our fellow-men are His test of our humility toward Him. May He teach us that our humility before Him is the only power that can enable us to be always humble with our

> *Perfect love finds its blessedness in blessing others.*

fellowmen. Our humility must be the life of Christ, the Lamb of God, within us.

Let all teachers of holiness, whether in the pulpit or on the platform, and all seekers after holiness, whether in the prayer closet or in the congregation, take warning. There is no pride so dangerous, none so subtle and insidious, as the pride of holiness. It is not that a man ever says, or even thinks, *"Come not near me; for I am holier than thou!"* No, indeed, the thought would be regarded with abhorrence. But there grows up, all unconsciously, a hidden habit of soul that feels complacency in its attainments. It cannot help seeing how far it is in advance of others. It can be recognized, not always in any special self-assertion or self-laudation, but simply in the absence of the deep self-abasement that is the mark of the soul that has seen the glory of God (Job 42:5–6; Isa. 6:5). It reveals itself, not only in words or thoughts, but in a tone—a way of speaking to others—in which those who have the gift of spiritual discernment cannot help but recognize the power of self. Even the world with its keen eyes notices it. The world points to it as a proof that the claim of a heavenly life does not bear any especially heavenly fruits.

Oh, brothers and sisters, let us beware! Unless we make the increase of humility our study, we may find that we have been delighting in beautiful thoughts and feelings, in solemn acts of consecration and faith, while the only sure mark of the presence of God—the disappearance of self—was missing the entire time. Come and let us flee to Jesus, and hide ourselves in Him until we are clothed with His humility. That alone is our holiness.

chapter 8

◆

Humility and Sin

Humility and Sin

Sinners; of whom I am chief.
—1 Timothy 1:15

H umility is often identified with penitence and contrition. As a consequence, there appears to be no way of fostering humility except by keeping the soul occupied with its sin. We have learned, I think, that humility is something else and something more. We have seen in the teaching of our Lord Jesus and in the Epistles how often the virtue is earnestly taught without any reference to sin. In the very nature of things—in the whole relationship of man to the Creator—in the life of Jesus as He lived it and imparts it to us, humility is the very essence of holiness and of blessedness. It is the displacement of self by the enthronement of God. Where God is all, self is nothing.

Though it is this aspect of the truth I have felt it especially necessary to emphasize, I hardly need to say what new depth and intensity man's sin and God's grace give to the humility of believers. We have only to look at a man like the apostle Paul to see how, through his life as a ransomed and holy man, the deep consciousness of having been a sinner lives inextinguishably.

We all know the passages in which Paul referred to his life as a persecutor and blasphemer. *"I am the least of the apostles, that am not meet to be called an apostle, because I persecuted the church of God....I laboured more abundantly than they all: yet not I, but the grace of God which was with me"* (1 Cor. 15:9–10). *"Unto me, who am less than the least of all the saints, is grace given, that I should preach among the Gentiles"* (Eph. 3:8). *"[I] was before a blasphemer, and a persecutor, and injurious: but I obtained mercy, because I did it ignorantly in unbelief....Christ Jesus came into the world to save sinners; of whom I am chief"* (1 Tim. 1:13, 15).

God's grace had saved Paul; God remembered his sins no more; but never, never could he forget how terribly he had sinned. The more he rejoiced in God's salvation, and the more his experience of God's grace filled him with unspeakable joy, the clearer was his consciousness that he was a saved sinner. And he was more aware that salvation had no meaning or sweetness except as the sense of his being a sinner made it precious and real to him. Never for a moment could he forget that it was a sinner whom God had taken up in His arms and crowned with His love.

> *You are a sinner whom God took into His arms with love.*

The Scriptures just quoted are sometimes referred to as Paul's confession of daily sinning. One has only to read them carefully in their context to see how little this is the case. They have a far deeper meaning. They refer to what lasts throughout eternity, and what will give its deep undertone of amazement and adoration to the humility with which the ransomed bow before the throne, as those who have been washed from their sins by the blood of the Lamb. Never, even in glory, can they be anything other than ransomed sinners. Never for a moment in this life can God's child live in the full light of His love without understanding that the sin out of which he has been saved is his one only right and title to all that grace has promised to do.

The humility with which he first came as a sinner acquires a new meaning when he learns how it suits him as a man. And then ever again, the humility in which he was born as a man has its deepest, richest tones of adoration in the memory of what it is to be a monument of God's wondrous, redeeming love.

The true significance of what these expressions of Paul teach us comes out all the more strongly when we notice the remarkable fact that, through his whole Christian course, we never find anything like a confession of sin. Not even in the Epistles, where he expounded on the most intensely personal admissions, did he confess his sins. Nowhere is there any mention of shortcoming or defect, nowhere any suggestion to his readers that he has failed in duty, or sinned against the law of perfect love.

On the contrary, there are many passages in which he vindicated himself in language that means nothing if it does not appeal to a faultless life before God and men.

"Ye are witnesses, and God also, how holily and justly and unblameably we behaved ourselves among you that believe" (1 Thess. 2:10). *"Our rejoicing is this, the testimony of our conscience, that in simplicity and godly sincerity,...and more abundantly to you-ward"* (2 Cor. 1:12). This is not an ideal or an aspiration. It is an appeal to what his actual life had been. However we may account for this absence of confession of sin, anyone will admit that it must point to a life in the power of the Holy Spirit such as is seldom realized or expected in our time.

The point that I wish to emphasize is this: the very fact of the absence of such confession of sinning only gives more force to the truth that the secret of deeper humility is not to be found in daily sinning. Rather, it is to be found in the habitual, never-for-a-moment-to-be-forgotten position, which the more abundant grace will keep more distinctly alive. Our true place—the only place of blessing, our one abiding position before God—must be that of those whose highest joy is to confess that they are sinners saved by grace.

Coupled with Paul's deep remembrance of having sinned so terribly in the past, before grace and the consciousness of being kept from present sinning had met him, was the abiding remembrance of the dark, hidden power of sin ever ready to come in, and only kept out by the presence and power of the indwelling Christ. *"In me (that is, in my flesh,) dwelleth no good thing"* (Rom. 7:18). These words describe the flesh as it is to the end. *"The law of the Spirit of life in Christ Jesus hath made me free from the law of sin and death"* (Rom. 8:2). This glorious deliverance is neither the annihilation nor the sanctification of the flesh, but a continuous victory given by the Spirit as He puts to death *"the deeds of the body"* (v. 13).

As health expels disease, light swallows up darkness, and as life conquers death, so the indwelling of Christ through the Spirit is the health and light and life of the soul. But with this, the conviction of our helplessness and danger always tempers our faith in this momentary and unbroken action of the Holy Spirit, giving us a chastened sense of dependence and making faith and joy the handmaids of humility. This humility lives only by the grace of God.

The three passages quoted on page seventy-six all show that it was the wonderful grace bestowed upon Paul, and for which he felt the need every moment, that humbled him so deeply. The grace of God that was with him enabled him to labor more abundantly than the others. The very nature and glory of grace for the sinner is the grace to preach to the heathen *"the unsearchable riches of Christ"* (Eph. 3:8). It is also the grace that was exceedingly abundant, with the faith and love that are in Christ Jesus (1 Tim. 1:14). It was this grace that kept Paul's consciousness of having once sinned, and being liable to sin, so intensely alive. *"Where sin abounded, grace did much more abound"* (Rom. 5:20). This reveals how the very essence of grace is to deal with and take away sin, and how it must always be so. The more abundant the experience of grace, the more intense the consciousness of being a sinner. It is not sin, but God's grace constantly

> *The indwelling of Christ is the health and life of the soul.*

reminding a man what a sinner he was, that will keep him truly humble. It is not sin, but grace, that will make me indeed know myself as a sinner, and make the sinner's place of deepest humility the place I never leave.

I fear that there are many who have sought to humble themselves by strong expressions of self-condemnation and self-denunciation, and yet have to confess with sorrow that a humble spirit, accompanied by kindness, compassion, meekness, and patience, is still as far off as ever. Being occupied with self, even amid the deepest self-abhorrence, can never free us from self. It is the revelation of God, not only by the law condemning sin, but by His grace delivering us from it, that will make us humble. The law may break the heart with fear. But it is only grace that works the sweet humility that becomes a joy to the soul as its second nature. It was the revelation of God in His holiness, drawing near to make Himself known in His grace, that made Abraham and Jacob, Job and Isaiah, bow so low. There will be no room for self in the soul that waits for, trusts, worships, and is filled with the presence of God the Creator as the all of man in his nothingness, and God the Redeemer as the all of the sinner in his sinfulness. Only in this way can the promise be fulfilled: *"The haughtiness of men shall be made low: and the* LORD *alone shall be exalted in that day"* (Isa. 2:17).

It is the sinner dwelling in the full light of God's holy, redeeming love—in the experience of that full indwelling of divine love, which comes through Christ and the Holy Spirit—who cannot be anything but humble. Not to be occupied with your sin, but to be occupied with God, brings deliverance from self.

chapter 9

———◆———

Humility and Faith

chapter 9

✦

Humility and Faith

How can ye believe, which receive honour
one of another, and seek not the honour
that cometh from God only?
—John 5:44

*I*n an address I heard recently, the speaker said that
the blessings of the higher Christian life were often
like the objects exposed in a shop window—one
could see them clearly and yet could not reach them.
If told to stretch out his hand and take, a man would
answer, "I cannot; there is a thick pane of glass between
me and them." Likewise, Christians may clearly see the
blessed promises of perfect peace and rest, of overflow-
ing love and joy, of abiding communion and fruitfulness,
yet feel that there is something hindering the true possession. And what might that be? Nothing but pride.

The promises made to faith are so free and sure,
the invitations and encouragements are so strong, and
the mighty power of God on which they may depend

is so near and free, that only something that hinders faith can hinder the blessing from being ours. In our text verse, Jesus discloses to us that it is indeed pride that makes faith impossible. *"How can ye believe, which receive honour one of another"*? As we see how pride and faith are irreconcilably at variance in their very natures, we will learn that faith and humility are one at their roots. We will learn that we can never have more of true faith than we have of true humility. We will see that we may indeed have strong intellectual conviction and assurance of the truth while pride is kept in the heart, but that these make a living faith—which has power with God—an impossibility.

We need only to think for a moment what faith is. Is it not the confession of nothingness and helplessness, the surrender and the waiting to let God work? Is it not in itself the most humbling thing there can be—the acceptance of our place as dependents, who can claim or get or do nothing but what grace bestows? Humility is simply the disposition that prepares the soul for living on trust. And even the most secret breathing of pride—in self-seeking, self-will, self-confidence, or self-exaltation—only serves to strengthen the self that cannot enter into the kingdom or possess the things of the kingdom, because it refuses to allow God to be what He is and must be—the all in all.

We must allow God to be what He is— the all in all.

Faith is the sense organ by which we perceive and understand the heavenly world and its blessings. Faith seeks the glory that comes from God—that only comes where God is all. As long as we take glory from one another, as long as we seek and love and jealously guard the glory of this life—the honor and reputation that come from men—we do not seek and cannot receive the glory that comes from God. Pride renders faith impossible. Salvation comes through a cross and a crucified Christ. Salvation is the fellowship with the crucified Christ in the Spirit of His cross. Salvation is union with, delight and participation in, the humility of Jesus. Is it any wonder that our faith is so feeble when pride still reigns so much, and we have hardly learned to long or pray for humility as the most necessary and blessed part of salvation?

Humility and faith are more nearly allied in Scripture than many people realize. See it in the life of Christ. There are two cases in which He spoke of a great faith. In the first instance, the centurion said, *"I am not worthy that thou shouldest come under my roof"* (Matt. 8:8). At this humility, Jesus marveled and replied, *"I have not found so great faith, no, not in Israel"* (v. 10). In the second case, the mother humbly spoke, *"Truth, Lord: yet the dogs eat of the crumbs which fall from their masters' table"* (Matt. 15:27). And the Lord answered her, *"O woman, great is thy faith"* (v. 28). It is the humility that brings a soul to be nothing before God that also removes every hindrance to faith. Humility makes the soul fear that it would dishonor Him by not trusting Him wholly.

Dear readers, do we not have here the cause of failure in the pursuit of holiness? Is it not this that made our consecration and our faith so superficial and so short-lived? We had no idea to what an extent pride and self were still secretly working within us. We were not aware of how God alone, by His incoming and His mighty power, could cast them out. We did not understand how nothing but the new and divine nature, entirely taking the place of the old self, could make us really humble. We did not know that absolute, unceasing, universal humil-

> *The cross, the death, and the grave are our path to glory.*

ity must be the root disposition of every prayer and every approach to God, as well as of every dealing with our fellowman. We did not realize that we might as well attempt to see without eyes, or live without breath, as believe or draw near to God or rest in His love without an all-pervading humility and lowliness of heart.

Have we not been making a mistake in taking so much trouble to believe, while all the time there was the old self in its pride seeking to take hold of God's blessing and riches? No wonder we could not believe. Let us change our course. Let us seek first of all to humble ourselves *"under the mighty hand of God, that he may exalt [us]"* (1 Pet. 5:6). The cross, the death, and the grave, into which Jesus humbled Himself, were His path to the glory of God. And they are our path. Let our one desire and our fervent prayer be to be humbled with Him and like Him. Let us gladly accept whatever can humble us before God or men—this alone is the path to the glory of God.

You perhaps feel inclined to ask a question. I have spoken of some who have blessed experiences, or are the means of bringing blessing to others, and yet are lacking in humility. You ask whether these do not prove that they have true, strong faith, even though they all too clearly seek the honor that comes from men.

More than one answer can be given. But the principal answer in our present context is this: they indeed have a measure of faith, in proportion to which, and with the special gifts bestowed upon them, is the blessing they bring to others. But in that very blessing, the work of their faith is hindered through the lack of humility. The blessing is often superficial or transitory just because they are not the nothing that opens the way for God to be all. A deeper humility would, without a doubt, bring a deeper and fuller blessing. The Holy Spirit not only working in them as a Spirit of power, but dwelling in them in the fullness of His grace—especially that of humility—would communicate Himself to them for a life of power, holiness, and steadfastness now seen all too little.

"How can ye believe, which receive honour one of another?" Brothers and sisters! Nothing can cure you of the desire to receive honor from men, or of the sensitivity and pain and anger that come when it is not given, except giving yourself to seek only the glory that comes from God. Let the glory of the all-glorious God be everything to you. You will be freed from the glory of men and of self, and be content and glad to be nothing. Out of this nothingness you will grow *"strong in faith, giving glory to God"* (Rom. 4:20). You will find that the deeper you sink in humility before Him, the nearer He is to fulfill every desire of your faith.

chapter 10

◆

Humility and Death to Self

chapter 10

◆

Humility and Death to Self

*He humbled himself, and became obedient
unto death, even the death of the cross.*
—Philippians 2:8

*H*umility is the path to death, because in death
it gives the highest proof of its perfection.
Humility is the blossom of which death to self is
the perfect fruit. Jesus humbled Himself unto death and
opened the path in which we, too, must walk. As there
was no way for Him to prove His surrender to God to the
very uttermost, or to give up and rise out of His human
nature to the glory of the Father, except through death,
so it is with us. Humility must lead us to die to self. We
must prove how wholly we have given ourselves up to it
and to God. Only in this way are we freed from fallen
nature and can we find the path that leads to life in
God, to the full birth of the new nature of which humility is the breath and the joy.

I have spoken of what Jesus did for His disciples when He communicated His resurrection life to them. In the descent of the Holy Spirit, He, the glorified and enthroned meekness, actually came from heaven Himself to dwell in them. He won the power to do this through death; in its innermost nature, the life He imparts is a life out of death. It is a life that has been surrendered to death and has been won through death. He who came to dwell in them was Himself One who had been dead and now lives forevermore. His life, His person, His presence bears the marks of death, of being a life begotten out of death.

This life in His disciples bears the death marks, too. Only as the Spirit of the death of the dying One dwells and works in the soul can the power of His life be known. The first and chief of the marks of the dying of the Lord Jesus—the death marks that show the true follower of Jesus—is humility. For these two reasons, only humility leads to perfect death. Only death perfects humility. Humility and death are in their very nature one. Humility is the bud; in death the fruit is ripened to perfection.

Humility Leads to Perfect Death

Humility means the giving up of self and becoming perfect nothingness before God. Jesus *"humbled himself, and became obedient unto death."* In death He gave the highest, the perfect proof of having given up His will to the will of God. In death He gave up His self, with its natural reluctance to drink the cup. He gave up the life He had in union with our human nature. He died to self and the sin that tempted Him, and, as man, He entered into the perfect life of God. If it had not been for His boundless humility, counting Himself as nothing except as a servant to do and suffer the will of God, He would never have died.

This gives us the answer to the question so often asked, and of which the meaning is so seldom clearly understood: how can I die to self? The death to self is not your work; it is God's work. In Christ you are dead to sin. The life that is in you has gone through the process of death and resurrection. You may be sure you are indeed dead to sin. But the full manifestation of the power of this death in your disposition and conduct depends on the measure in which the Holy

> *Death to self is not your work; it is God's work through Christ.*

Spirit imparts the power of the death of Christ. And it is here that the teaching is needed. If you want to enter into full fellowship with Christ in His death, and know the full deliverance from self, humble yourself. This is your one duty.

Place yourself before God in your utter helplessness. Consent heartily to the fact of your weakness to slay or make yourself alive. Sink down into your own nothingness, in the spirit of meek and patient and trustful surrender to God. Accept every humiliation, look upon every person who tries your patience or irritates you as a means of grace to humble you. Use every opportunity of humbling yourself before your fellowmen as a help to remain humble before God. It is by the mighty strengthening of His Holy Spirit that God reveals Christ fully in you. In this manner, Christ, in His form of a servant, is truly formed in you and dwells in your heart. God will accept such humbling of yourself as the proof that your whole heart desires it. He will accept it as your very best prayer for it, and as your preparation for His mighty work of grace. It is the path of humility that leads to perfect death, the full and perfect experience that we are dead in Christ.

Death Leads to Perfect Humility

Only this death leads to perfect humility. Oh, beware of the mistake so many make who would like to be humble but are afraid to be too humble. They have so many qualifications and limitations, so many reasonings and questionings, as to what true humility is to be and to do, that they never unreservedly yield themselves to it. Beware of this. Humble yourself to the point of death. It is in the death of self that humility is perfected. You can be sure that at the root of all real experience of more grace, of all true advance in consecration, of all actually increasing conformity to the likeness of Jesus, there must be a deadness to self that proves itself to God and men in our dispositions and habits.

It is sadly possible to speak of the death-life and the Spirit-walk while even the tenderest love sees how much there is of self. The death to self has no surer death-mark than a humility that makes itself *"of no reputation"* (Phil. 2:7), that empties out self and takes the form of a servant. It is possible to speak much and honestly of fellowship with a *"despised and rejected"* Jesus (Isa. 53:3), and of bearing His cross, while the meek, lowly, kind, and gentle humility of the Lamb of God is not seen—is scarcely sought. The Lamb of God means two things—meekness and death. Let us seek to receive Him in both forms. In Him they are inseparable; they must be in us also.

What a hopeless task if we had to do the work! Nature can never overcome nature, not even with the help of grace. Self can never cast out self, even in the regenerate man. Praise God! The work has been done, finished, and perfected forever. The death of Jesus, once and forever, is our death to self. And the ascension of Jesus, His entering once and forever into the Holiest, has given us the Holy Spirit to communicate to us in power, and makes the power of the death-life our very own. As the soul, in the pursuit and practice of humility, follows in the steps of Jesus, its consciousness of the need of something more is awakened. Its desire and hope is quickened; its faith is strengthened; and it learns to look up and claim and receive that true fullness of the Spirit of Jesus. That fullness can daily maintain His death to self and sin in its full power, and make humility the all-pervading spirit of our lives. (See Note C on page 119.)

"Know ye not that so many of us as were baptized into Jesus Christ were baptized into his death?" (Rom. 6:3). *"Likewise reckon ye also yourselves to be dead indeed unto sin, but alive unto God through Christ Jesus our Lord....Yield yourselves unto God, as those that are alive from the dead"* (vv. 11, 13). The whole self-consciousness of the Christian is to be characterized by the Spirit that animated the death of Christ. He has to ever present himself to God as one who has died in Christ, and in

Christ is alive from the dead, *"always bearing about in [his] body the dying of the Lord Jesus"* (2 Cor. 4:10). His life ever bears the twofold mark: its roots striking in true humility deep into the grave of Jesus, the death to sin and self, and its head lifted up in resurrection power to the heaven where Jesus is.

Believer, claim in faith the death and the life of Jesus as yours. Enter, in His grave, into rest from self and its work—the rest of God. With Christ, who committed His spirit into the Father's hands (see Luke 23:46), humble yourself and descend each day into that perfect, helpless dependence on God. God will raise you up and exalt you.

Every morning, sink in deep, deep nothingness into the grave of Jesus. Every day, the life of Jesus will be manifested in you. Let a willing, loving, restful, happy humility be the sign that you have indeed claimed your birthright—the baptism into the death of Christ. *"By one offering he hath perfected for ever them that are sanctified"* (Heb. 10:14). The souls that enter into His humiliation will find in Him the power to see and consider self dead, and, as those who have learned and received of Him, will walk with all lowliness and meekness, supporting one another in love. The death-life is seen in a meekness and humility like that of Christ.

chapter 11

◆

Humility and Happiness

chapter 11

◆

Humility and Happiness

Most gladly therefore will I rather glory in my infirmities,
that the power of Christ may rest upon me. Therefore I
take pleasure in infirmities....For when I am
weak, then am I strong.
—2 Corinthians 12:9–10

*I*n case Paul should exalt himself, by reason of the exceeding greatness of the revelations he had received from God, he was sent a thorn in the flesh to keep him humble. Paul's first desire was to have it removed, and three times he asked the Lord that it might depart. The answer came that the trial was a blessing; that, in the weakness and humiliation it brought, the grace and strength of the Lord could be better manifested. Paul at once entered into a new stage in his relationship to the trial. Instead of simply enduring it, he most gladly gloried in it. Instead of asking for deliverance, he took pleasure in it. He had learned that the place of humiliation is the place of blessing, power, and joy.

Virtually every Christian passes through these two stages in his pursuit of humility. In the first stage, he fears and flees and seeks deliverance from all that can humble him. He has not yet learned to seek humility at any cost. He has accepted the command to be humble and seeks to obey it, though only to find out how utterly he fails. He prays for humility, at times very earnestly. But in his secret heart, he prays more—if not in word, then in wish—to be kept from the very things that will make him humble. He is not yet so in love with humility as the beauty of the Lamb of God, and the joy of heaven, that he would sell all to procure it. In his pursuit of it, and his prayer for it, there is still somewhat of a sense of burden and of bondage. To humble himself has not yet become the spontaneous expression of a life and a nature that are essentially humble. It has not yet become his joy and only pleasure. He cannot yet say, "Most gladly do I glory in weakness; I take pleasure in whatever humbles me."

> *Pleasure in humility comes with revelation of the Lord Jesus.*

But can we hope to reach the stage in which this will be the case? Undoubtedly. And what will it be that brings us there? That which brought Paul there—a new revelation of the Lord Jesus. Nothing but the presence of God can reveal and expel self. A clearer insight was given to Paul into the deep truth that the presence of Jesus will banish every desire to seek anything in ourselves and will make us delight in every humiliation that prepares us for His fuller manifestation. Our humiliations lead us, in the experience of the presence and power of

Jesus, to choose humility as our highest blessing. Let us try to learn the lessons the story of Paul teaches us.

We may have advanced believers, eminent teachers, and men of heavenly experiences, who have not yet fully learned the lesson of perfect humility, gladly glorying in weakness. We see this in Paul. The danger of exalting himself was coming very near. He did not yet know perfectly what it was to be nothing; to die, so that Christ alone might live in him; to take pleasure in all that brought him low. It appears as if this were the highest lesson that he had to learn—full conformity to his Lord in that self-emptying where he gloried in weakness so that God might be all.

The highest lesson a believer has to learn is humility. Oh, that every Christian who seeks to advance in holiness may remember this well! There may be intense consecration and fervent zeal and heavenly experience, and yet, if it is not prevented by very special dealings of the Lord, there may be an unconscious self-exaltation with it all. Let us learn the lesson—the highest holiness is the deepest humility. Let us remember that it does not come by itself, but only as it is made a matter of special dealing on the part of our faithful Lord and His faithful servant.

Let us look at our lives in the light of this experience and see whether we gladly glory in weakness, whether we take pleasure, as Paul did, in trials, necessities, and distresses. Yes, let us ask whether we have learned to regard a reproof, just or unjust, a reproach from friend or enemy, trouble or difficulty into which others bring us, as, above all, an opportunity of proving how Jesus is all to us. It is an opportunity to prove how our own pleasure and honor are nothing, and how humiliation is truly what we take pleasure in. It is indeed blessed—it is the deep happiness of heaven—to be so free from self that whatever is said about us or done to us is lost and swallowed up in the thought that Jesus is all.

Let us trust Him who took charge of Paul to take charge of us, too. Paul needed special discipline and special instruction to learn what was more precious than even the unutterable things he had heard in heaven—what it is to glory in weakness and lowliness. We need it, too—oh, so much. He who cared for Paul will care for us, too. He watches over us with a jealous, loving care, lest we exalt ourselves. When we are exalting ourselves, He seeks to disclose to us the evil, and to deliver us from it. In trial and weakness and trouble, He seeks to bring us low until we learn that His grace is all. And until we learn to take pleasure in the very thing that brings us and keeps us low. His strength made perfect in our weakness, His presence filling and satisfying our emptiness, becomes the secret of a humility that need never fail. This humility can, in full sight of what God works in and through us, always say, as Paul did, *"In nothing am I behind the very chiefest apostles, though I be nothing"* (2 Cor. 12:11). His humiliations had led him to true humility, with its wonderful gladness and glorying and pleasure in all that humbles.

"Most gladly therefore will I rather glory in my infirmities, that the power of Christ may rest upon me. Therefore I take pleasure in infirmities." The humble man has learned the secret of abiding gladness. The weaker he feels, the lower he sinks, and the greater his humiliations appear, the more the power and the

presence of Christ are his portion. Then, as he says, *"I be nothing"* (2 Cor. 12:11), the Word of his Lord brings ever deeper joy: *"My grace is sufficient for thee"* (v. 9).

I feel as if I must once again sum up everything in these two lessons: the danger of pride is greater and nearer than we think, and the grace for humility is also.

The Danger of Pride

The danger of pride is greater and nearer than we think, especially at the time of our richest experiences. The preacher of spiritual truth with an admiring congregation hanging on his words, the gifted speaker on a holiness platform expounding the secrets of the heavenly life, the Christian giving testimony to a blessed experience, the evangelist moving on in triumph and made a blessing to rejoicing multitudes—no man knows the hidden, the unconscious danger to which these are exposed. Paul was in danger without knowing it. What Jesus did for him is written for our admonition, so that we may know our danger and know our only safety. Let it be said no more that one who teaches or professes holiness is full of self or that he does not practice what he preaches or that his blessing has not made him humbler or gentler. Jesus, in whom we trust, can make us humble.

> *Pride is nearer than we think, but so is the grace for humility.*

The Grace for Humility

Yes, the grace for humility is greater and nearer, too, than we think. The humility of Jesus is our salvation.

Jesus Himself is our humility. Our humility is His care and His work. His grace is sufficient for us (see 2 Cor. 12:9) to meet the temptation of pride, too. His strength will be perfected in our weakness (v. 9). Let us choose to be weak, to be low, to be nothing. Let humility be joy and gladness to us.

Let us gladly glory and take pleasure in weakness—in all that can humble us and keep us low. The power of Christ will rest upon us. Christ humbled Himself; therefore God exalted Him (Phil. 2:8–9). Christ will humble us and keep us humble. Let us heartily consent; let us trustfully and joyfully accept all that humbles. The power of Christ will rest upon us. We will find that the deepest humility is the secret of the truest happiness, of a joy that nothing can destroy.

chapter 12

———◆———

Humility and Exaltation

chapter 12

◆

Humility and Exaltation

He that humbleth himself shall be exalted.
—Luke 14:11

Humble yourselves in the sight of the Lord,
and he shall lift you up.
—James 4:10

Humble yourselves therefore under the mighty hand of
God, that he may exalt you in due time.
—1 Peter 5:6

*J*ust yesterday I was asked the question, How am I to conquer this pride? The answer was simple. Two things are needed. Do what God says is your work; humble yourself. Trust Him to do what He says is His work; He will exalt you.

The command is clear: humble yourself. This does not mean that it is your work to conquer and cast out the pride of your nature and to form within yourself the lowliness of the holy Jesus. No, this is God's work, the very essence of the exaltation in which He lifts you up into the real likeness of the beloved Son. What the command does mean is this: take every opportunity of humbling yourself before God and man. Humble yourself and stand persistently, not withstanding all failure and falling, under this unchanging command. Do this with faith in the grace that is already working in you and in the assurance that more grace will be available for the victory that is coming. Look to the light that conscience flashes on the pride of the heart and its workings.

Accept with gratitude everything that God allows from within or without, from friend or enemy, in nature or in grace, to remind you of your need of humbling, and to help you to it. Believe humility to indeed be the highest virtue, your very first duty before God, and the one perpetual safeguard of the soul. Set your heart upon it as the source of all blessing. The promise is divine and sure: *"He that humbleth himself shall be exalted."* See that you do the one thing God asks: humble yourself. God will see that He does the one thing He has promised. He will give more grace; He will exalt you in due time.

All God's dealings with man are characterized by two stages. There is the time of preparation, when command and promise—with the mingled experience of effort and inability, of failure and partial success, with the holy expectancy of something better that these awaken—train and discipline men for a higher stage. Then comes the time of fulfillment, when faith inherits the promise and enjoys what it had so often struggled for in vain. This law holds good in every part of the Christian life and in the pursuit of every separate virtue. This is because it is grounded in the very nature of things.

In all that concerns our redemption, God must take the initiative. When that has been done, man's turn comes. In the effort toward obedience and attainment, he must learn to know his weakness. In self-despair, he must learn to die to himself, and so be voluntarily and intelligently equipped to receive the promise from God. The Father will complete what man had accepted at the beginning in ignorance. So God, who had been the beginning before man rightly knew Him or fully understood what His purpose was, is longed for and welcomed as the end—as the all in all.

It is the same in the pursuit of humility. To every Christian the command comes from the throne of God Himself: humble yourself. The earnest attempt to listen and obey will be rewarded—yes, rewarded—with the painful discovery of two things. The one is the depth of pride—unwillingness to consider oneself and to be considered nothing, to submit absolutely to God—that existed, that one

The command comes from the throne of God: humble yourself.

never knew. The other is what utter weakness there is in all our efforts, and also in all our prayers for God's help, to destroy the hideous monster. Blessed is the man who now learns to put his hope in God and to persevere, notwithstanding all the power of pride within him, in acts of humility before God and men.

We know the law of human nature: acts produce habits, habits breed dispositions, dispositions form the will, and the rightly-formed will is character. It is not any different in the work of grace. As acts, persistently repeated, beget habits and dispositions, and these strengthen the will, He who works *"both to will and to do"* (Phil. 2:13) comes with His mighty power and Spirit. The humbling of the proud heart, with which the penitent saint casts himself so often before God, is rewarded with the *"more grace"* (James 4:6) of the humble heart, in which the Spirit of Jesus has conquered and brought the new nature to its maturity. In this heart, He, the meek and lowly One, now dwells forever.

"Humble yourselves in the sight of the Lord, and he shall lift you up." He will exalt you. And of what does this exaltation consist? The highest glory of man is in being only a vessel, to receive and enjoy and show forth the glory of God. Man can do this only as he is willing to be nothing in himself so that God may be all. Water always fills the lowest places first. The lower, the emptier a man lies before God, the speedier and the fuller the inflow of the divine glory will be.

The exaltation God promises is not, cannot be, any external thing apart from Himself. All that He has to give or can give is only more of Himself, to take more complete possession. The exaltation is not, like an earthly prize, something arbitrary, in no necessary connection with the conduct to be rewarded. No, but it is in its very nature the effect and result of the humbling of ourselves. It is nothing but the gift of a divine indwelling humility—a conformity to and possession of the humility of the Lamb of God—which equips us for fully receiving the indwelling of God.

"He that humbleth himself shall be exalted." Jesus Himself is the proof of the truth of these words. He is the pledge of the certainty of their fulfillment to us. Let us take His yoke upon us and learn from Him, for He is *"meek and lowly in heart"* (Matt. 11:29). If we are willing to stoop to Him, as He has stooped to us, He will yet stoop to each one of us again, and we will find ourselves equally yoked with Him. As we enter deeper into the fellowship of His humility, and either humble ourselves or bear the humbling of men, we can count on the Spirit of His exaltation, *"the spirit of glory and of God"* (1 Pet. 4:14), to rest upon us. The presence and the power of the glorified Christ will come to those who are of a humble spirit.

When God can again have His rightful place in us, He will lift us up. Make His glory your main concern in humbling yourself. He will make your glory His concern in perfecting your humility, and breathing into you, as your abiding life, the very Spirit of His Son. As the all-pervading life of God possesses you, there will be nothing so natural and nothing so sweet as to be nothing, with not a thought or wish for self, because all is occupied with Him who fills all. *"Most gladly therefore will I rather glory in my infirmities, that the power of Christ may rest upon me"* (2 Cor. 12:9).

> *When God can have His rightful place in us, He will lift us up.*

Fellow believers, do we not have here the reason why our consecration and our faith have availed so little in the pursuit of holiness? It was by self and its strength that the work was done under the name of faith. It was for self and its happiness that God was called in. It was, unconsciously, but still truly, in self and its holiness that the soul rejoiced. We never knew that humility—absolute, abiding, Christlike humility, pervading and marking our entire lives with God and man—was the most essential element of the life of the holiness we sought.

It is only in the possession of God that I lose myself. In the height and breadth and glory of the sunshine, the littleness of a particle of dust is seen playing in the sunlight. In the same way, humility is our being, in God's presence, nothing but specks dwelling in the sunlight of His love.

> How great is God! how small am I!
> Lost, swallowed up in Love's immensity!
> God only there, not I.

May God teach us to believe that to be humble, to be nothing in His presence, is the highest attainment and the fullest blessing of the Christian life. He speaks to us: *"I dwell in the high and holy place, with him also that is of a contrite and humble spirit"* (Isa. 57:15). May this be our destiny!

> Oh, to be emptier, lowlier,
> Mean, unnoticed, and unknown,
> And to God a vessel holier,
> Filled with Christ, and Christ alone!

Final Words

Until the spirit of the heart is renewed, until it is emptied of all earthly desires and stands in a habitual hunger and thirst after God—which is the true spirit of prayer—all our prayer will be too much like lessons given to scholars. We will mostly say them only because we dare not neglect them. But do not be discouraged. Take the following advice, and then you may go to church without any danger of mere lip service or hypocrisy, even though there is a hymn or a prayer whose language is higher than that of your heart. Do this, go to the church as the tax collector went to the temple. Stand inwardly in the spirit of your mind in the form that he outwardly expressed when he cast down his eyes and could only say, *"God be merciful to me a sinner"* (Luke 18:13). Stand unchangeably, at least in your desire, in this form or state of heart. It will sanctify every petition that comes out of your mouth. When anything is read or sung or prayed that is more exalted than your heart is, make this an occasion of further sinking down in the spirit of the tax collector. You will then be helped and highly blessed by the prayers and praises that seem only to belong to a heart better than yours.

This, my friend, is a secret of secrets. It will help you to reap where you have not sown, and it will be a continual source of grace in your soul. For everything that inwardly stirs in you, or outwardly happens to you, becomes a real good to you if it finds or excites in you this humble state of mind. For nothing is in vain, or without profit, to the humble soul. It stands always in a state of divine growth; everything that falls upon it is like a dew of heaven to it. Shut yourself up, therefore, in this form of humility. All good is enclosed in it; it is a water of heaven that turns the fire of the fallen soul into the meekness of the divine life and creates the oil out of which the love of God and man gets its flame. Always be enclosed in it—let it be as a garment with which you are always covered. Breathe nothing but in and from its spirit. See nothing but with its eyes. Hear nothing but with its ears. And then, whether you are in the church or out of the church, hearing the praises of God or receiving wrongs from men and the world, all will be edification, and everything will help your growth in the life of God move forward.

Notes

Notes

---◆---

- *Note A*

All this is to make it known that pride can degrade the highest angels into devils, and humility can raise fallen flesh and blood to the thrones of angels. Thus, this is the great end of God's raising a new creation out of a fallen kingdom of angels. For this reason, it stands in its state of war between the fire and pride of fallen angels, and the humility of the Lamb of God. It is here that the last trumpet may sound the great truth throughout the depths of eternity: that evil can have no beginning but from pride, and no end but from humility.

The truth is this: pride must die in you, or nothing of heaven can live in you. Under the banner of the truth, give yourself up to the meek and humble spirit of the holy Jesus. Humility must sow the seed, or there can be no reaping in heaven. Do not look at pride as only an unbecoming temper, or at humility as only a decent virtue. The one is death, and the other is life; the one is all hell, the other is all heaven.

As much as you have of pride within you, so you have of the fallen angel alive in you. As much as you have of true humility, so you have of the Lamb of God within you. If you could see what every stirring of pride does to your soul, you would beg of everything you meet to tear the viper from you, though it may mean the loss of a hand or an eye. If you could see what a sweet, divine, transforming power there is in humility, how it expels the poison of your nature and makes room for the Spirit of God to live in you, you would rather wish to be the footstool of all the world than lack the smallest degree of it.

- *Note B*

"We need to know two things: first, that our salvation consists wholly in being saved from ourselves, or that which we are by nature; and second, that in the whole nature of things, nothing could be this salvation or savior to us but such a humility of God as is beyond all expression. Hence, the first unalterable condition given by the Savior to fallen man is this: Unless a man denies himself, he cannot be My disciple (Matt. 16:24). Self is the whole evil of fallen nature; self-denial is our capacity of being saved. Humility is our savior. Self is the root, the branches, the tree, of all the evil of our fallen state. All the evils of fallen angels and men have their birth in the pride of self. On the other hand, all the virtues of the heavenly life are the virtues of humility. It is humility alone that bridges the impassable gulf between heaven and hell. What is then, or in what lies, the great struggle for eternal life? It lies entirely in the battle between pride and humility. Pride and humility are the two master powers—the two kingdoms at war for the eternal possession of man.

"There never was, and never will be, but one humility, and that is the one humility of Christ. Pride and self have the all of man, until man has his all from Christ. Therefore, he only fights the good fight that is fought so that the self-idolatrous nature he has from Adam may be brought to death by the supernatural humility of Christ brought to life in him." —William Law

• *Note C*

"To die to self or to come from under its power is not, cannot be, done by any active resistance we can make to it by the powers of nature. The one true way of dying to self is the way of patience, meekness, humility, and resignation to God. This is the truth and perfection of dying to self. For if I ask you what the Lamb of God means, must you not tell me that it means the perfection of patience, meekness, humility, and resignation to God? Must you not therefore say that a desire and faith in these virtues is an application to Christ, is a giving up of yourself to Him and the perfection of faith in Him? And then, because this inclination of your heart to sink down in patience, meekness, humility, and resignation to God is truly giving up all that you are and all that you have from fallen Adam, it is leaving all you have to follow Christ. It is your highest act of faith in Him. Christ is nowhere but in these virtues. When they are there, He is in His own kingdom. Let this be the Christ you follow.

"The Spirit of divine love can have no birth in any fallen creature until it wills and chooses to be dead to all self in a patient, humble resignation to the power and mercy of God.

"I seek all my salvation through the merits and mediation of the meek, humble, patient, suffering Lamb of God. He alone has the power to bring forth the blessed birth of these heavenly virtues in my soul. There is no possibility of salvation but in and by the birth of the meek, humble, patient, resigned Lamb of God in our souls. When the Lamb of God has brought forth a real birth of His own meekness, humility, and full resignation to God in our souls, then it is the birthday of the Spirit of love in our souls. Whenever we attain this, our souls will feast with such a peace and joy in God that the remembrance of everything that we called peace or joy before will be blotted out.

"This way to God is infallible. This infallibility is grounded in the twofold character of our Savior: first, as He is the Lamb of God, a principle of all meekness and humility in the soul; and second, as He is the Light of heaven, and blesses eternal nature, and turns it into a kingdom of heaven. When we are willing to get rest for our souls in meek, humble resignation to God, then He, as the light of God and heaven, joyfully breaks in upon us. He turns our darkness into light and begins the kingdom of God and of love within us that will never have an end." —William Law

A Prayer for Humility

A Prayer for Humility

Here I will give you an infallible touchstone that will tie everything to the truth. It is this: retire from the world and all conversation, only for one month. Neither write, nor read, nor debate anything with yourself. Stop all the former workings of your heart and mind. And, with all the strength of your heart, stand for the entire month, as continually as you can, in the following form of prayer to God. Offer it frequently on your knees. But whether sitting, walking, or standing, be always inwardly longing and earnestly praying this one prayer to God:

"Lord, I pray that of Your great goodness You would make known to me, and take from my heart, every kind and form and degree of pride, whether it be from evil spirits, or my own corrupt nature; and that You would awaken in me the deepest depth and truth of the humility that can make me capable of Your light and Holy Spirit."

Reject every thought, except that of waiting and praying in this matter from the bottom of your heart, with the kind of truth and earnestness that is used by people in torment who wish to pray and be delivered from it. If you can and will give yourself up in truth and sincerity to this spirit of prayer, I will venture to affirm that, if you had twice as many evil spirits in you as Mary Magdalene had, they will all be cast out of you, and you will be forced with her to weep tears of love at the feet of the holy Jesus.

About the Author

◆

Andrew Murray

A ndrew Murray (1828–1917) was an amazingly prolific Christian writer. He lived and ministered as both a pastor and author in the towns and villages of South Africa. Some of Murray's earliest works were written as an extension of his pastoral work to provide nurture and guidance to Christians, whether young or old in the faith. Once books such as *Abide in Christ, Divine Healing,* and *With Christ in the School of Prayer* were written, Murray became widely known, and new books from his pen were awaited with great eagerness throughout the world.

He wrote to give daily practical help to many of the people in his congregation who lived out in the farming communities and could only come into town for church services on rare occasions. As he wrote these books of instruction, Murray adopted the practice of placing many of his more devotional books into thirty-one separate readings to correspond with the days of the month.

At the age of seventy-eight, Murray resigned from the pastorate and devoted most of his time to his manuscripts. He continued to write profusely, moving from one book to the next with an intensity of purpose and a zeal that few men of God have ever equaled. He often said of himself, rather humorously, that he was like a hen about to hatch an egg; he was restless and unhappy until he got the burden of the message off his mind.

During these later years, after hearing of pocket-sized paperbacks, Andrew Murray immediately began to write books to be published in that fashion. He thought it was a splendid way to have the teachings of the Christian life at your fingertips, where they could be carried around and read at any time of the day.

One source has said of Andrew Murray that his prolific style possesses the strength and eloquence that are born of deep earnestness and a sense of the solemnity of the issues of the Christian life. Nearly every page reveals an intensity of purpose and appeal that stirs men to the depths of their souls. Murray moves the emotions, searches the conscience, and reveals the sins and shortcomings of many of us with a love and hope born out of an intimate knowledge of the mercy and faithfulness of God.

For Andrew Murray, prayer was considered our personal home base from which we live our Christian lives and extend ourselves to others. During his later years, the vital necessity of unceasing prayer in the spiritual life came to the forefront of his teachings. It was then that he revealed the secret treasures of his heart concerning a life of persistent and believing prayer.

Countless people the world over have hailed Andrew Murray as their spiritual father and given credit for much of their Christian growth to the influence of his priceless devotional books.

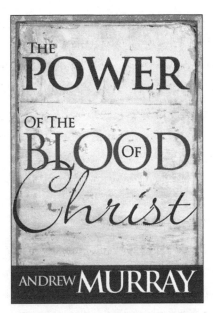

The Power of the Blood of Christ
Andrew Murray

Sure, you know that "there's power in the blood," just like the old hymn says—but are you actually experiencing that power in your daily life? Instead, are you feeling spiritually tired? Worn-out? Weak? Lifeless? Walking in your own strength instead of relying on the finished work of Christ can leave you spiritually exhausted and emotionally weary. Join Andrew Murray in this classic exploration of the blessings to be found in Christ's blood. As you delve deep into this work, you will discover the joy of forgiveness through Christ's blood like never before and experience amazing breakthroughs as you daily abide in the victory secured by His blood. Get ready to enjoy the Christian life like never before. Get ready to walk in *The Power of the Blood of Christ*!

ISBN: 978-0-88368-242-5 • Trade • 176 pages

WHITAKER
HOUSE

www.whitakerhouse.com

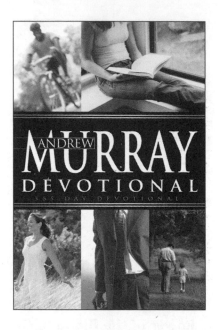

Andrew Murray Devotional
Andrew Murray

Andrew Murray's uplifting messages for each day of the
year will comfort and refresh you in your walk with God.
Spending time with God daily will bring a new joy and peace
into your life. As you daily explore these truths from Andrew
Murray, you will connect with God's glorious power and
see impossibilities turn into realities. Your prayer life will be
transformed. You will experience the joy of seeing powerful
results in your life as you minister to others. Don't miss out
on the most important part of the day—your miraculous,
life-changing moments spent with the Creator.

ISBN: 978-0-88368-778-9 • Trade • 400 pages

WHITAKER
HOUSE

www.whitakerhouse.com